Do I Belong in Seminary?

Ronald E. Parker

An Alban Institute Publication

Library of Congress Catalog Card 98-72483
ISBN 1-56699-201-X

07   06   05   04   03   WP   2   3   4   5   6   7   8   9   10   11

TABLE OF CONTENTS

I. Why am I reading this book?

I'm assuming that you are not reading these words in the waiting room of your dentist's office. I assume that you have this book in your hand and have opened it to the first page of the first chapter because the question "Do I belong in seminary?" is of some interest to you. Maybe you are experiencing a vague dissatisfaction with the direction in which your life is going. Maybe you have a specific and powerful sense that you do, in fact, belong in seminary. Maybe you are wondering why anyone would be interested in being in seminary.

Perhaps right now you are beginning to feel a little nervous. Actually, I wouldn't be surprised if you are thinking of looking for a grocery bag to make a plain cover for this book so no one will see you reading it and start making assumptions about you. This is natural. (To make a cover for this book, cut the grocery bag open and lay it flat, then lay the book on the bag, mark the size and cut a piece of paper large enough to go all the way around the book and fold inside each cover. Don't tape the cover to the book yet. You may start to get a little more comfortable with the idea of seminary.)

Anyway, here are some likely reasons you or anyone else might be reading this book.

1. Someone gave it to you

If the folks at the Alban Institute, who published this book, are right, some of you are reading it at the suggestion of someone else: a pastor, a friend, a family member. It doesn't mean you have never thought about seminary before. A surprising number of people have. It's just that it often takes a nudge from someone else to take the step of considering it seriously. Maybe that other person has seen something in you that you haven't yet seen in yourself. This is worth your consideration. You are fortunate if you have such a friend who wants to support you on your life journey.

2. You are choosing a vocation

Most people who write books about ministry throw around the words "vocation" and "call" as if everyone knows what they are talking about. The fact is, those words are not much in vogue in the popular culture. So just bear with me for a moment and see if you grasp why these concepts are important.

Both of these words suggest that what we do with our lives is not merely a matter of personal choice. The novelist Hermann Hesse has his character Damian say: "I realize today that nothing in the world is more distasteful to a man than to take a path that leads to himself." Some part of who we are becoming draws us beyond ourselves. Frankly, most of us don't hear God's voice booming out of a cloud or a burning bush. But there are people and things and situations that "speak" to us in ways that change the direction of our lives. So strictly speaking, we don't choose a vocation; it chooses us.

The "voc" in vocation is about a voice. It comes from the Latin word *vocare* which means a summons. You may experience this call coming from somewhere deep within. You may hear it in the voice of another person. You may hear it in some great need that calls to you. You may hear it in a gift of yours that is not being used. Wherever you experience it, your vocation calls you beyond what you may have thought of by yourself. Second Isaiah has God say it this way: "For my thoughts are not your thoughts, neither are your ways my ways.... For as the heavens are higher than the earth, so are my ways higher than your ways and my thoughts higher than your thoughts" (Isaiah 55:8-9).

Wait! Don't close the book yet. I know this is suddenly sounding very pious and ministerial. But vocations are not the private property of ministers. Vocations are for everyone, even if seminary isn't. Later in this book, I'll have more to say about some of the specific callings that lead people to seminary. Right now, I'd like to head you off if you think that feeling called to something larger automatically means going to seminary. It doesn't.

Because talk about vocation and calling have so often been tied to ordained ministry, you may think that if you feel called, you should be in seminary preparing for ordination. You could just as legitimately be called to be an attorney or in business or to be a teacher or an engineer. All of those can take you beyond yourself. All of those are ways to give something to others.

Therefore, reading this book might help you to decide not to go to seminary.

3. You are thinking of changing jobs

A vocation is not a career. A career is pretty much all about you. We all know what a "car" is. It turns out the word "career" originally meant something like a highway or a race track. It may be that the particular race track you are on has been feeling like it is meant for a common kind of rodent. That may be why you are reading this book.

We all need some way to earn a living. We hope that the work we do is satisfying and productive. Our vocation is bigger than our job, but deciding to change jobs could be leading you to seminary. This book may help you decide if seminary will prepare you for the work you want to do. It won't necessarily help you choose a job or get one. Sorry.

4. You want to grow spiritually

Warning: "grow" almost always means "challenge" as well. If by "growing spiritually" you mean confirming what you already believe, you'll be better off finding a cozy congregation of like-minded people and trying to avoid thinking new thoughts. There is hardly any seminary worth its salt that won't challenge your faith on the way to strengthening and deepening it. Every step forward involves letting go of something from your past. This isn't easy, but it's worth it.

The primary work of seminary education is to engage in critical reflection on the scriptures, traditions, and experience of a particular faith community. Beliefs are analyzed and explored in relation to the situations in which they originally arose as well as in terms of the contemporary contexts in which they are practiced. You will encounter people of diverse beliefs and backgrounds all engaged in this struggle together. This process enriches your own faith.

5. You have a friend in seminary and it sounds interesting

Many people who find themselves in seminary never thought of it until a friend or someone in their church decided to go to seminary. Then the possibility became real. You may be reading this book because of some stirrings that were created by a friend telling of his or her experience in seminary. You are fortunate, first of all, because you have an informant you trust, and second because you have a way of imagining what a seminary experience would be like. You might want to take the opportunity to visit your friend at school and get a firsthand look.

6. You know someone else who might consider seminary

One alternative to covering this book with a plain brown wrapper is to assure anyone who might ask that you are reading it so you can help a friend decide about seminary. This, of course, might be true. You might really want to help a friend or spouse or parent or child of yours decide about seminary. Or you might be kidding yourself.

Seriously, churches have an important role in guiding people who are considering seminary. Pastors and laypeople in churches need to be informed about the kinds of people needed in spiritual leadership and the paths they take in preparation. Every member of a faith community should be looking around for someone who might need encouragement in this direction. This book could help you know how to guide others who are considering seminary.

7. You already know you are going to seminary and need more information

I've spent a lot of years talking to people who are considering seminary and I have heard many of the same questions asked again and again. This book tries to address some of those questions or tell you where to go for answers. The best advice I can give you is don't be afraid to ask, even if the questions seem elementary. You almost certainly have the same questions that other prospective seminary students are asking. Trust me on this.

Note: You don't have to read the whole book

My third grade teacher scolded me for skipping around in my textbooks and not finishing what I started. I was saddled with that idea until one of my seminary professors told me that most books aren't worth reading cover to cover. I encourage you to read the sections of this book that seem to speak to your situation. Skip the others. I can't imagine that every chapter would be relevant to every person (except the author, of course).

I once heard the Dalai Lama speak to about 10,000 students at the University of California, Berkeley. After a lovely talk in which he pronounced many wise and profound things, he commented, "I hope you have found something helpful in what I have said, but if you haven't, just forget about it." Treat this book that way. It's your life, not mine or anyone else's.

II. Who goes to seminary?

1. People preparing for ordained ministry

You may have thought that these are the only people in seminary. Certainly the largest number of seminary students are those preparing for ordained parish ministry. The actual percentage varies from school to school depending on the breadth of degrees offered as well as the flexibility of the M.Div. (Master of Divinity) curriculum. If you are planning to be ordained in a mainline denomination, then seminary is generally a necessity.

2. People preparing for professional lay ministry

In the past two or three decades churches have begun to place an increased emphasis on the ministry of the laity. This means that more and more people enroll in seminary who have no intention of being ordained, but plan to serve in some professional capacity in the church. Lay professionals may work in education, administration, music, youth or children's ministries, community outreach, or a host of other ministries.

3. People preparing for volunteer lay ministries

While some seminary students will seek full-time employment in congregations, some intend to engage in ministry as volunteers. Some of these people are retired. One man I know was able to retire at the age of 50 and attend seminary. He spent the next 20 years living on his retirement income and offering his services free to a variety of churches and out-reach ministries. Some attending seminary will continue in their current jobs with a new sense of that work as a church ministry. These people are seeking skills in theological reflection and a spiritual foundation for their work.

4. People preparing for community ministries

In my experience, one of the fastest growing groups of people attending seminary today is those who intend to enter a ministry of social service or advocacy through a community organization or non-profit agency. With the decrease in government services and the increased pressure for nonprofit organizations to take over those services, many are finding opportunities for ministry in this area.

Why, you ask, would someone attend seminary instead of a school of social work or public administration? Good question. One woman who had spent many years as an educational consultant was now plan-ning to start a charter school in a poor area of a large city. She said, "I knew I needed to go back to school in preparation. I could have gone back for a doctorate in education; I could have gone for an M.B.A.; but I chose to go to seminary because I knew that the most important thing in this school would be the spiritual values at its foundation."

Social-service providers are increasingly aware of a need for spiri-tual foundations in their work. Even when you work in a setting where faith or a particular faith is not explicitly part of the organization, your faith will be at the foundation of your own work. Understanding your work as ministry may change it from a career to a vocation.

5. People preparing for academic careers

Some M.Div., M.A., and M.T.S. (Master of Theological Studies) stu-dents plan to go directly on to a Ph.D. program. In those seminaries that offer doctoral programs, there will also, of course, be doctoral students. In most cases, these students are more interested in the academic side of the curriculum than in issues of practical ministry. On the other hand, even though they are probably going to teach, some may plan to be ordained, especially if they intend to teach in a seminary. These will most likely pursue the M.Div. degree.

6. People exploring their call to ministry

You may picture seminary as a collection of single-minded, clearly committed people who are certain of the direction in which God is calling them. There probably are a few like that, but they are the exception rather than the rule. Most find themselves continuing the process of discernment throughout their seminary education. The currents of call run deeper than we can plumb at any one point in life. Call changes as circumstances and opportunities change and as our own skills develop. No matter how certain you are at any time of your life, you should always be open to this exploration.

While seminaries are designed to serve those who have a definite direction in mind, many students use a year or two of seminary education as a way of testing their call. Some seminaries encourage this kind of student more than do others and may even have special programs to support their exploration. Other seminaries may privately bemoan the fact that there are too many "searchers" in seminary. Encouraged or not, these students will always be a part of the seminary landscape.

7. People who want to deepen and enrich their faith

As thoughtful laypeople take their faith more seriously, many of them find that they want to go beyond the study opportunities offered by their local churches. Some of them take a course or two in seminary. Others enroll in a degree program to receive a more structured and comprehensive theological education. Many people who have recently come to church as adults did not grow up in the church and did not have the Christian education earlier generations experienced. These new participants often have a thirst for a deeper knowledge of their faith. Some of them turn to seminaries. Such people bring fresh questions and a vital connection between everyday life and the classroom.

8. People augmenting their current vocations

As people try to make their faith more a part of their work, some of them decide that they need more education. A psychotherapist realizes that spiritual issues are at the core of many of her clients' problems, so she goes to seminary for a year to increase her skills in spiritual direction. An English professor wants a better understanding of the religious issues in the literature he teaches. A journalist decides to shift his work to covering religious issues. A professional musician is taking on a ministry of music in a local church. A nurse has been appointed to the ethics panel in her hospital and wants to study issues of bio-ethics and faith. A businessman wants to reflect on the ethics of his business. All these and more may find theological study helpful in the work they already do.

9. People still unclear about their reasons for being in seminary

Frankly, there are some people in seminaries who, in spite of the seminary's admissions process and their own efforts, don't seem to know for sure why they are there. You don't really want to be one of these people; the demands are too great and it costs too much.

III. Am I called?

The short answer is "yes." I hinted earlier that call is not limited to those entering ordained ministry. In fact, Christians believe that we are all called by virtue of our baptism. Your call is about your total way of being in the world as well as the work you do. Ordained clergy have no corner on it.

Malcolm Warford (a former seminary president) puts it this way,

> For too long we have discussed the nature of vocation in a way that only applies to the professions, but God calls us at far more significant levels of meaning than can be identified with certain roles in society. There are no occupations that in themselves are sanctified as expressions of calling. It is the ends toward which any work is directed that determine whether or not it is a form of love and a means of service.[1]

1. The first question

In the summer of 1977, three other fathers and I, each of us with two sons, rented a houseboat for an excursion on the waters of the Sacramento River. It was the kind of adventure that fathers are supposed to have with their sons. The older boys, who ranged in age up to 14, caught the spirit of the adventure and occupied themselves with swimming, diving, fishing, steering the boat, and a multitude of adventurous games they invented. My son Nathan, who was four and the youngest, didn't get the spirit of the adventure. At that stage of his life his idea of adventure was a trip down the spiral slide at the local kiddy park.

As the adventure wore on and Nathan wore out, he began to follow me around in his oversize and uncomfortable life jacket asking that ageless question of children in the summertime: "Daddy, what can I do?" Dutifully, I thought up as many interesting activities as I could, but one morning, after what seemed like the 50th time I had heard that question, I responded in exasperation, "Nothing!" Then Nathan, with the innocent profundity of a four-year-old, said, "Then why am I here?"

It was one of those questions that cuts to the heart of things. It challenged my motivations for bringing him along, the meaning of father-son relationships, and indeed, the meaning of life itself.

It's a question that all of us eventually ask. In the midst of feeling dragged along on a life adventure by a parent or some other force whose motivations we don't really understand, and after struggling day in and day out to figure out what we are supposed to do, one day in our frustration, we shout back at life, "Then why am I here?" The answer to that question—whether it comes thundering out of the sky or welling up within, whether it comes from the highest ecclesiastical authority or a four-year-old child—the answer to that question is our call. It is our *vocation*, putting into words the reason for our unique being in this particular time and place in history.

Some people seem to feel no need of knowing or even believing that there is a reason for their being—a "why" to their existence. For them, finding interesting activities to do is enough. But most of us who go to seminary, or even consider it, do ask this question, at least occasionally, if not incessantly. Certainly persons who decide to seek ordination will be forced to clarify, examine, and trot out for committees and boards of ministry their understanding of their call. It is picked at, examined, and criticized until that question becomes a refrain in the candidate's head: "Then why am I here?"

The story is often told of three stone masons who were asked what they were doing. One said he was cutting stones. The second said he was making a wall. The third said he was building a cathedral. In the same way, one person may say, "I'm putting in my time," another, "I'm doing my job," while another performing the same work may say, "I'm serving God." The difference is knowing why we are here.

2. You are here

We all start somewhere. It's the "here" in the question, "Why am I here?" Because your call rises up from this givenness of your existence, a clear perception and acceptance of where you find yourself is an essential first step in understanding your call. There are at least three aspects of the place you find yourself that play important roles in your call: the social context in which you live and have been formed, the historical community in which you stand, and the particular gifts that you have been given.

First of all, your call is the natural conclusion of the context in which you were born and have been formed. The philosopher Michael Polanyi has described one's calling as the context out of which one thinks and acts. He says that a person's calling is constituted by the biological and cultural rootedness of all responsible actions.

> No one can transcend his [or her] cultural milieu very far, and beyond this [one] must rely on it uncritically. I consider that this matrix of my thought determines my personal calling.[2]

You were born with particular genes, of a particular race or culture, and into a place and time in history. This particular givenness of your existence is the context of your calling.

Of course, some situations are more compelling than others. It is not uncommon for a call to occur in some extraordinary need in the world which moves you to answer the why of your existence in ways you had not expected. Abigail Adams wrote in a letter to Thomas Jefferson: "Great necessities call forth great leaders."[3] That may be true for you.

Your call also takes place in the context of an historical community of faithfulness. In the oldest part of the Old Testament we read:

> When your children ask you in time to come, "What is the meaning of the decrees, and the statutes, and the ordinances that the Lord our God has commanded you?" then you shall say to your children, "We were Pharaoh's slaves in Egypt, but the Lord brought us out of Egypt with a mighty hand. The Lord displayed before our eyes great and awesome signs and wonders against Egypt, against Pharaoh and all his household. He brought us out from there in order to bring us in, to give us the land that he promised on oath to our ancestors. Then

the Lord commanded us to observe all these statutes, to fear the Lord our God, for our lasting good, so as to keep us alive, as is now the case. (Deuteronomy 6:20-24)

That is the way the earliest part of the tradition shared by Jews, Christians, and Muslims put it. Maybe you wouldn't use the same kind of language, but your own call is informed by your encounter with the historical tradition of which you are a part. Understanding how others in your tradition have received and responded to God's call will inform your own call.

In other words, the story of how you got here is essential to your understanding of why you are here. In the television miniseries based on Alex Haley's *Roots*, the fact that Kunta Kinte knows he is an African warrior and not a slave makes all the difference in how he lives his life. His daughter, Kizzy, explaining why she cannot marry a man she has come to love, says, "He's not like us. Nobody ever told him where he came from, so he doesn't know where he is going." Knowing where you've come from is an essential ingredient in knowing where you're going and the meaning of where you are right now.

When you study scriptures and read your own people's history, you find yourself drawn into a way of perceiving and acting that has continuity with those who have gone before you. Seeing the world through your tradition creates the context for your calling. That is an important part of seminary work.

A third part of the given foundation of your call is the particular constellation of gifts that you come with. Paul writes in his first letter to the Corinthians:

Now there are varieties of gifts, but the same Spirit; and there are varieties of services, but the same Lord; and there are varieties of activities, but it is the same God who activates all of them in everyone. To each is given the manifestation of the Spirit for the common good. (1 Corinthians 12:4-7)

Or we read in 1 Peter,

Like good stewards of the manifold grace of God, serve one another with whatever gift each of you has received. (1 Peter 4:10)

Perhaps you find identifying your own gifts difficult. Of course, the presence or absence of some gifts is obvious. I am five feet six inches tall, which to me is a pretty clear indication that I am not called to play professional basketball. On the other hand, don't be shy. What are you naturally good at? What do you find fulfilling? Sometimes this gift does not naturally match up with some occupation you know about. You may be challenged to find a place to exercise the gift you have been given, but the fact remains that this gift is part of the foundational context of your call.

Elizabeth O'Connor of Church of the Savior in Washington, D.C. writes,

> Because our gifts carry us out into the world and make us partici-
> pants in life, the uncovering of them is one of the most important
> tasks confronting any one of us. When we talk about being true to
> ourselves—being the persons we are intended to be—we are talking
> about gifts. We cannot be ourselves unless we are true to our gifts.
> When we talk about vocation, whether we are artists or engineers,
> we are talking about gifts. In a discussion about commitment, we
> are on the same subject for the place of our concrete involvement is
> determined by our gifts. Serious reflection on almost any aspect of
> our lives leads into a consideration of gifts.[4]

3. Don't just sit here

You are here, but you are not stuck here. The other side of this given context is your response. If there is only givenness, there is no freedom or responsibility.

When I call up the stairs to tell my son that dinner is ready, I do it in anticipation of a response. When I don't get one, I call again. The response is usually, "Just a minute." This helps us see the difference between call and necessity. If I go upstairs and grab him by the scruff of the neck and drag him downstairs, that is not call but necessity. I know that there are people who speak of God's call and God's will as if it were necessity, but this lets them escape taking responsibility for their own decisions.

So call happens in the dynamic interaction between the place where you find yourself and your own response. The language of call is different from the language of identity. Identity asks, "Who am I?" Call asks, "How shall I respond?"

The biblical scholar, Walter Brueggemann, distinguishes between vocation and identity. He sees vocation as based on the metaphor of the covenant between you and God. The covenant captures the two sides of call and response. Brueggemann says:

> ...such a view of reality *transposes all identity questions into vocational questions.* The notion of identity questions is based on the assumption that the person, in and of himself/herself has within his/her body an identity to be embraced. Identity questions are, by definition, self-focused. But we have urged on the basis of our governing metaphor [the covenant] that the premise itself is wrong because the human person is not self-grounded and therefore does not have within himself/herself the essentials for accepting or arriving at an identity. Rather, identity for a person is given in the call of the other One. It is the voice of the initiating One who calls human persons to a destiny. Maturation is coming to terms in free ways with the givenness of God's purpose in our lives.[5]

In this sense, then, your vocation is the ordering of your whole life in response to God's call and purposes. Understanding the meaning of your life in terms of the covenant means that you are constantly responding to the givenness of your life in terms of God's call. There is nothing static about vocation. It is a dynamic process which is described in the unfolding of your life. You can respond in faith or unfaith, but the call is new in each moment.

Second Isaiah has God saying: "For my thoughts are not your thoughts, neither are your ways my ways.... For as the heavens are higher than the earth, so are my ways higher than your ways and my thoughts higher than your thoughts" (Isaiah 55:8-9). Brueggemann comments on this passage:

> Biblical anthropology is from the beginning *missional.* Biblical faith asserts that being grounded in this other One who has purposes that are not our purposes characterizes our existence as missional, that is as claimed for and defined by the One who gives us life. The metaphor of the covenant poses the central reality of our life in terms of

vocation. Vocation means we are called by this One who in calling us to *be* calls us to *service*. And in that comes freedom.[6]

In other words, gifts are for giving.

4. The gift must move

Lewis Hyde writes about the nature of gifts in the culture of the American Indian. He says the principle is that

> ...whatever we have been given is supposed to be given away again, not kept. Or, if it is kept, something of similar value should move on in its stead, the way a billiard ball may stop when it sends another scurrying across the felt, its momentum transferred.... As it is passed along, the gift may be given back to the original donor, but this is not essential.... The only essential is this: *the gift must always move.* There are other forms of property that stand still, that mark a boundary or resist momentum, but the gift keeps going.[7]

Elizabeth O'Connor puts it this way:

> Each one of us has an irrevocable vocation to be Christ, and the Christ that we are called to be is irreplaceable. It has to be my vision of Christ and, if I do not fulfill that, there is going to be something missing forever and forever in the [Realm] of Heaven....[8]

If you want to test your call, take the gifts that you have been given and begin to look for places to give them. Make them move.

5. Your passion and the world's needs

I once counseled with a man who told me he knew that he was called to ordained ministry. He told me that he hated doing all of the things that ministers do, that there was not one aspect of it he could imagine enjoying. Nevertheless, he was certain that he was called. I failed to convince him otherwise, though I tried.

The experience of meeting with him over a period of months and struggling to help him see that God was most likely calling him in a different direction helped me to see the way in which we have often distorted God's call. Somehow we have promoted the idea in the church that there is some special virtue in doing things that we hate doing and are not particularly good at. The more we dislike it, the more likely God is calling us to do it. (I had a Sunday school teacher once who felt that way about Sunday school teaching. It was a disaster.) This idea sometimes even leads people to pretend that they don't like doing things that they love to do so that they can feel virtuous for doing them. Crazy, isn't it? Would God call you to something that made you unhappy?

The fact is, however, God uses your joys and desires to call you. Joseph Campbell captures this side of call when he says, "Follow your bliss." That may not be the whole story, but I do not believe God calls us to lives that have no joy in them. In fact, I believe that God uses your passion to call you. Are you beginning to see the two-sided nature of call? Where you find yourself/how you respond; what you have been given/what you can give; where you find joy/what the world needs. Where these opposites come together is where you find your call. A few paragraphs by the writer Fredrick Buechner have captured this point so well that you will find them quoted in nearly every book on call or vocation written in the past 20 years. Not to be left out, I quote these words for you now:

> There are all kinds of voices calling you to all different kinds of work, and the problem is to find out which is the voice of God rather than of society, say, or the Superego, or Self-Interest.
>
> By and large a good rule for finding out is this. The kind of work God usually calls you to is the kind of work (a) that you need to do and (b) that the world needs to have done. If you really get a kick out of your work, you've presumably met requirement (a), but if your work is writing TV deodorant commercials, the chances are you've missed requirement (b). On the other hand, if your work is being a doctor in a leper colony, you have probably met requirement (b), but if most of the time you're bored and depressed by it, the chances are you have not only bypassed (a) but probably aren't helping your patients much either.
>
> Neither the hair shirt nor the soft berth will do. The place God

calls you is the place where your deep gladness and the world's deep hunger meet.[9]

This does not mean, however, that responding to your call or giving your gifts will be easy. Deep joy and the easy path are not the same thing. Responding to your call will be frightening, costly, and take great faith. Elizabeth O'Connor suggests the following exercise:

> When you have named your talents or gifts, list the risks that you have to take in order to actualize them. What will you have to give up if you are to develop these gifts? What are the obstacles that you foresee?[10]

Are you willing to take these risks?

6. Confirmed in community

Besides finding call in your given context, in your historical community, in your gifts, in the needs of the world, and in your deep joy, your call also comes through your relationships with other people—your participation in community. You cannot see your call as purely personal, in isolation from other people. I remember a Jules Feiffer cartoon where a person is saying:

> I meet people with friendly smiles and shiny eyes, who tell me they're happy because they've found the "word" and they all have different "words" but identical friendly smiles and identical shiny eyes—which don't focus on me but on their word and the more they smile and shine, the more I feel I don't exist. Someday I'll find my word. I hope it involves a second person.

Call always involves other people in at least two ways. First, they may voice a call that we had not heard. Let me tell you how I was called to ministry. When I was a senior in high school, I was active in the Methodist Youth Fellowship at the district and conference level. I came to know many of the ministers in the Detroit Conference and came to be known by them. One day after a district meeting, a minister named Charlie Beynon said, "Have you ever thought about going into the ministry?" I hadn't, but now a word of invitation had been spoken and it began to ring true for me. For the longest time I thought that God didn't call me into the ministry, but that Charlie did. In retrospect, I have to say that if I had not heard God's call in Charlie's words, I might not have responded in the same way.

The other way in which a call involves other people is through confirmation. This is most visible and explicit with candidates for ordination—much to their discomfort, I must say. When someone comes to the church saying they are called to ordained ministry, the church says, "Let's see if we agree." The various committees and structures, interviews and examinations that candidates for ordination must go through are the church's way of embodying its belief that a call is not just an individual matter. It is confirmed and nurtured in community. This may feel like an unnecessary and stressful burden; but when it is done well, it is a gift to your own process of discerning your call.

Though the structures are not usually so explicit, all of us need some sort of external confirmation of our call. You may need intentionally to seek out other people who can help you evaluate your gifts and the possible contexts in which they can make a contribution.

7. Coming home

Perhaps the final and most powerful confirmation of your call is a sense of finding a home. Sometimes this is a discovery of a new kind of work that concludes a long process of discernment. On the other hand, hearing your call may be no more than seeing in a new light what you are already doing. The poet T. S. Eliot puts it this way,

> With the drawing of this Love
> and the voice of this Calling
> We shall not cease from exploration
> And the end of all our exploring
> Will be to arrive where we started
> And know the place for the first time.[11]

8. Some straight talk about parish ministry

Having spent 17 immensely satisfying years as a parish pastor and loving
almost every day of it, I still feel compelled to issue a disclaimer—because I am acutely aware that many people choose this path not knowing
what they are getting into. You need a realistic picture of the demands
and difficulties of any vocation you choose, but nowhere is this more
important than in pastoral ministry. When you tell people in your church
that you are considering entering parish ministry, they will very likely
look on you with a sense of awe (except for those who think you have
lost your mind). In spite of the cynicism of many pastors, there is still a
good deal of romanticizing about ministry. If you are considering parish
ministry, you should be clear about what you are signing up for. So think
of the rest of this chapter as truth in advertising.

First of all, consider the personal qualities and professional skills
that parish ministry requires. Here is one denomination's estimate of the
qualities you will need:

> 1. High (but not rare) intellectual ability 2. High self-esteem and
> self-acceptance 3. Open, affirming, flexible relational style that
> produces effective communication 4. Ability to nurture faith in
> people 5. Ability to handle conflict, accept differences, and admit
> weaknesses 6. Commitment to the faith and the church 7. Demon-
> strated ability to care for individuals and the broader community
> 8. Willingness to serve without needing to be appreciated by others
> 9. Responsibility in task fulfillment 10. Ability to accept opposition
> without retaliation or discouragement 11. Commitment to recruiting
> and training laity in specific aspects of mission.[12]

How does this list sound to you? You are not required to have all these
strengths right now, but you have to be willing to struggle for them. This
list suggests that ministry is more than a body of knowledge and a bag of
tricks. It requires substantial spiritual, intellectual, and emotional gifts.

Parish ministry requires a solid spiritual foundation. You will not
survive unless you are undergirded by a strong sense of God's presence
on which you can call in the midst of schedules that often seem too full
for prayer. I once heard the missionary E. Stanley Jones voice the traditional adage that he spent an hour in prayer every day, except on those

days when he had an unusually full schedule; then he spent two hours. You, too, will need a regular discipline of staying in touch with God. You need to love doing this and take on the discipline willingly. Otherwise, it won't happen and you will find yourself on your own and exhausted.

Parish ministry also requires intellectual gifts. It calls you to study and teach. You are expected to have mastered the history and theology of your church and the skills of biblical interpretation. Seminary is graduate-level education and an intellectual challenge. If this kind of intellectual work is not for you, maybe seminary is not either. Ministry requires good intentions and a love of God, but not everyone with good intentions and a love of God is cut out for the intellectual challenges of ordained ministry.

Emotional strength is also essential. You will be expected to deal with the most intense experiences of life: birth, love, marriage, family, loss, and death. Being able to encompass these experiences emotionally is certainly essential to one entering this ministry. Also, because of your unique position of leadership in a spiritual community, people will project onto you the best and the worst they can imagine. They will have such high expectations of you that you will inevitably disappoint them. Then they will be angry with you. They will compare you with a beloved pastor from the past who is larger than life in their memory and whose failings they have forgotten. On the other hand, many will want to have a special friendship with you. Some will urge you to cross sexual boundaries. How will you handle the feelings that go with all of these situations?

Few jobs involve your essential identity more than does parish ministry. In addition to accomplishing tasks and communicating ideas, your person is very much a part of your ministry. The positive side of this is that your whole person is involved in your work, creating congruity between who you are and what you do. On the other hand, there will be times when the role does not fit so well. People will want you to be things that don't fit who you are. You (and probably your family) will feel like you are on display and maybe even on trial much of the time. You need to ask yourself whether you can handle this kind of visibility. It does not have to be destructive, but it is not for everyone. It takes a solid sense of yourself and a graceful manner of maintaining your own integrity in the face of conflicting demands.

Dealing with conflict is another of the challenges parish ministry brings. Churches are loving communities, places of peace and refuge; but they also have a way of getting into terrible conflicts. You will want to develop skills in helping communities manage conflict, but that is not enough. Conflict in the church will take a toll on you personally. Do you do well in the midst of conflict?

Maintaining realistic boundaries of time and work is another of the challenges you will face. Parish ministry offers you a field of unlimited possibilities. The needs of your community, let alone the world, are infinite. New ideas for programs and activities present themselves daily. On the other hand, you are one person and, assuming that you don't have to sleep, you have only seven 24-hour days a week. Parish ministry requires a person who knows how to set priorities and say "no." Otherwise it will consume you.

Setting these limits is made more complicated by the fact that you cannot, in fact, work 24 hours a day seven days a week. Establishing boundaries that take care of yourself is more difficult than simply saying there is no time. You have to be able to say to yourself and others, "In spite of the great needs of my community and the world, I am taking the day off to relax at the beach." You need to be able to do that with confidence and self-acceptance without sounding desperate or angry. Some ministers (and others) develop a style of going around looking like they are on the edge of exhaustion in order to justify taking a little time off. If you are on the edge of exhaustion, you have waited too long for the time off and you are modeling an unhealthy way of being in the world.

One of the joys of parish ministry is that it offers a wonderfully varied range of activities and opportunities. If you love learning new skills and taking on challenges that you have not prepared for, you will love it. On the other hand, the breadth of parish demands can drive you crazy. Sometimes you feel like you will never know enough. You are a marriage counselor, a scholar, a spiritual advisor, an administrator of a complex organization, a conflict manager, a social activist, an expert in finances, and, if you are in a small church you have to know how to fix the copy machine and unclog a toilet.

There was a time when the pastor of a church was automatically one of the most respected people in the community. This is not true anymore. Sorry about that. One writer puts it this way:

> Given our society's fascination with high technology, rapid change, and social management, the servant role model has fallen on hard

times. .... If clergy are portrayed on television at all, they are often shown as good, but generally ineffective, naive people who have no impact on society and are often taken advantage of by others. These weak, secondary characters often need to be rescued by a "hero" who is a rugged individualist, working outside the system to bring about justice and to right the wrongs of society.[13]

You will not thrive in the parish if you are counting on your position to confer a level of status and self-esteem that you do not carry within yourself.

If you have a spouse or partner and children, life in the parish will affect them as well. While congregations are increasingly comfortable with spouses who have their own careers and the need for family privacy, old traditions die hard. The best way to meet this challenge is to be sure that you and the other members of your family agree on the boundaries you will keep. Your spouse's career, your children's needs for your attention, and the necessity of family time away from the spotlight are crucial to good family health.

Finally, where are you willing to live? Some denominations are more flexible than others. One fact to consider is that many people come to ministry from large urban churches and then find themselves in their first assignment in a small rural parish. That's where the entry-level positions are. Can you imagine yourself here? These small churches bring hard financial realities. You will not be paid a high salary. If you are coming to ministry from another occupation, you will most likely experience a cut in salary. Can you cope with this?

Having said all this, I need to say once more that parish ministry is one of the most exciting, stimulating, and satisfying jobs there is. It offers you the privilege of accompanying people at the most private and deep moments of their lives. The variety of activities and occasions for creativity are endless. The opportunities for your own personal growth are unparalleled in any other occupation.

I recommend it, but enter with your eyes wide open.

IV. What do seminaries do?

1. Theological education vs. religious studies

If you want to study about various religions or religion in general, you should probably choose a university or college religious studies or religion department rather than a seminary. A seminary may have a course or two in comparative religion or a faculty member from a faith tradition other than its own. But most seminaries have been founded primarily for the purpose of training leaders for faith communities of one, or at most a few, denominations or religious perspectives. Thus the assumption is that teaching and learning take place within that tradition.

As a general rule, you go to a religious studies or religion department in a college or university to study *about* various religions, while you go to a seminary to study and reflect on your own religious faith. Theological or seminary education presupposes the student's engagement in the educational process as an adherent or practitioner of the seminary's faith perspective. A religious studies or religion department, on the other hand, assumes that all religious faiths will be treated more or less equally and that the teacher is not necessarily an adherent of the religion about which he or she is teaching. Of course, no one comes to the study of religion without a perspective or even set of practices of his or her own, but in a religious studies department, faculty members attempt to set that perspective aside in the name of objectivity.

A theological school starts with a faith perspective. Students and faculty engage in reflection on the traditions and practices of that faith with whatever appropriate tools are available. That does not mean that they ignore the tools and methods of modern scholarship used in the religious studies department, but that they use these tools and methods for the purpose of enhancing their understanding of their own faith traditions.

You are not necessarily unwelcome in a seminary if you come from a faith tradition different from the seminary's, but you have to enter the seminary with the understanding that you cannot demand "equal treatment" or "equal time" for all religions or faiths. If you are not a Christian, you may still choose to attend a Christian seminary for what you could learn there. But it is not legitimate to complain, as one student I know did, that there is too much talk about Jesus in the New Testament class. This being said, even denominational seminaries are having to adjust to more diverse student bodies than in the past.

There are also many nondenominational or multidenominational seminaries. Many of these seminaries, especially those which are more theologically and culturally liberal, make a more conscious effort to foster a diverse environment. On the other hand, there are some seminaries that are non-denominational, in that they are not tied to a particular church body, but still have a very specific, and sometimes even narrow, theological perspective. You will have to do your own investigation beyond the official designation of the seminary.

When considering a seminary, you should think carefully about the compatibility of your own faith with that of the seminary. How broad is the seminary's perspective? How flexible are you?

2. Academic study and professional training

Seminary education exists in a tension between academic scholarship and the practices of faith communities. For the most part, this is a creative tension. This tension derives from the belief in most churches that their leaders should be academically trained as well as prepared for the specific practices of ministry. While theological reflection and academic study inform and reform the concrete practices of ministry, the concrete contexts of ministry are the fertile soil out of which innovative academic work grows.

Seminaries and churches, as well as seminary professors and ministers, stand at a variety of places along the continuum between academic study and religious practice. Some churches do not require any academic training at all and are, in fact, suspicious of those who are academically trained. Others see this academic training as primary to the preparation of a minister.

You will find this tension across the whole curriculum and in individual courses within the seminary. Some courses will focus more on purely academic or theoretical issues, while others will be more about the practice of the faith and ministry. Depending on your own goals, you may find yourself drawn more to one approach than the other. While most seminaries try to maintain a balance between practical engagement and critical reflection, you will find that balance manifested differently at each seminary.

3. Degree programs

The Association of Theological Schools of the United States and Canada (ATS) is the primary accrediting agency for seminaries and has established standards for the degrees offered by theological schools. Each school has its own particular version of those degrees, and no one school offers all of the degrees accredited by ATS. The best way to develop an understanding of a particular seminary's degree programs is by reading the requirements in its catalog and talking to staff, faculty, and students. Following is a general outline of many typical seminary degrees as they are described in the ATS standards for accreditation.

Basic Programs Oriented Toward Ministerial Leadership:

Master of Divinity (M.Div.) The Master of Divinity degree is the normative degree to prepare persons for ordained ministry and for general pastoral and religious leadership responsibilities in congregations and other settings. It is the required degree for admission to the Doctor of Ministry degree program, and the recommended first theological degree for admission to advanced programs oriented to theological research and teaching.

Master of Religious Education (M.R.E.), Master of Christian Education (M.C.E.), Master of Arts in Religious Education (M.A. in Religious Education), Master of Arts in Christian Education (M.A. in Christian Education) The primary purpose of degrees with these various titles is to equip persons for competent leadership in various forms of educational ministry in congregations and other religious institutions.

Master of Arts in [specialized ministry] (M.A. in) The primary purpose of degrees that ATS designates as M.A. in (area of specialization) is to equip persons for competent leadership in some form of specialized ministry in congregations and other settings. The degree program may focus, for example, on youth ministry, counseling, missions, or social ministries.

Master of Church Music (M.C.M), Master of Sacred Music (M.S.M), Master of Music in Church Music (M.M. in Church Music), Master of Arts in Church Music (M.A. in Church Music) The purpose of these degrees is to equip persons for competent leadership in church or sacred music in congregations or other settings.

Basic Programs Oriented Toward General Theological Studies

Master of Arts (M.A.), Master of Arts (Religion)(M.A.R.), Master of Arts (Theological Studies) (M.A. in Theological Studies), Master of Theological Studies (M.T.S.) The purpose of these degree programs is to provide a basic understanding of theological disciplines for further graduate study or for general educational purposes.

Advanced Programs Oriented Toward Ministerial Leadership

Doctor of Ministry (D.Min.) The purpose of the Doctor of Ministry degree is to enhance the practice of ministry for persons who hold the M.Div. degree and have engaged in ministerial leadership.

Advanced Programs Primarily Oriented Toward Theological Research and Teaching

Master of Theology (Th.M.), Master of Sacred Theology (S.T.M.) The purpose of this degree is to provide a fuller mastery of one area or discipline of theological study than is normally provided at the M.Div. level. The program may serve a variety of aims: further graduate study at the doctoral level, preparation for some forms of teaching, the scholarly enhancement of ministerial practice, or disciplined reflection on a specialized function of ministry.

Doctor of Philosophy (Ph.D.), Doctor of Theology (Th.D.) These degree programs are intended primarily to equip persons for vocations of teaching and research in theological schools, colleges, and universities, or for the scholarly enhancement of ministerial practice. The same overall aims and standards apply to both the Ph.D. and the Th.D.; the nomenclature differs according to the history of its use in a particular school.[1]

4. Kinds of courses

While seminaries are graduate schools and presuppose a general liberal arts background at the bachelor's level, they still offer introductory courses in all of their areas of study. These introductory courses don't require that you have had preparation in that field already. So, for example, while a course in introduction to the Old Testament is taught at the graduate level, it is still an introduction and does not presuppose that you have ever had an Old Testament course before.

The traditional disciplines taught in seminaries are Scripture, history of Christianity, theology, and ethics. Most seminaries also offer courses oriented to the specific practices of ministry such as preaching, pastoral counseling, religious education, and worship. Growing out of these basic fields, many seminaries have developed specialties of their own such as religion and the arts, sociology of religion, feminist studies, biomedical ethics, church music, and ministry and theology within particular ethnic or cultural contexts. Denominational seminaries also offer courses specific to preparation for ministry in that particular church.

The degree programs of some seminaries are very structured, with mostly required courses. Others offer flexible programs with many electives. You should think carefully about which environment will help you most in meeting your goals.

5. Spiritual and vocational formation

"Formation" is a word often used to describe the ways seminaries and churches participate in a person's spiritual and vocational development. Formation may be addressed in specific classes or may take the form of working with a person called a "spiritual director." It may happen in small groups designed for this purpose. It will most certainly be part of your denominational process if you are seeking ordination. You will also want to find your own ways, with both peers and mentors, to work on your own development.

Because seminaries are preparing people for leadership in faith communities, they focus attention on your development as a person of faith in a way that a secular university does not. This is especially so in the degree programs designed to prepare for ministry while less so in the more purely academic programs. Some seminaries place greater emphasis on the development of the person than others do. A denominationally related seminary will place emphasis on formation in that particular tradition. Interdenominational schools may place less emphasis on formation in the curriculum but encourage students to seek this part of their preparation within their own church tradition.

Vocational development is usually an important aspect of field education and internship experiences. In your field placement you have an opportunity to try on the roles and practices of leadership and develop your own capacities and skills. Many seminaries require a classroom component to the field education experience in which students study topics related to their field setting and engage in theological reflection on their experience. In addition to addressing the practice of ministry, these classes may be places of intense vocational exploration.

6. Challenging faith/nurturing faith

Thinking critically about your faith challenges many things you have accepted uncritically in the past. While the purpose of this critical thinking is to deepen and strengthen your faith, sometimes it doesn't feel that way. Nearly every person who comes to seminary with a strong faith finds that faith shaken at some time during her or his time in seminary (usually about the fifth week of the first semester).

However, you will also find resources to nurture you during that time, so that the shaking of your foundations ultimately strengthens them. Fellow students who are experiencing the same struggles provide supportive companions on this difficult journey. They are probably the most important resource. Maintaining your relationship with a faith community outside the seminary also helps you integrate your new learnings. You still need a pastor of your own. Some courses and faculty members are better than others at nurturing faith in the midst of critical deconstruction. Identifying these and using them for support helps maintain your balance. Finally, the seminary may provide people such as campus chaplains, deans of students, academic advisors, and others to attend specifically to the nurturing of faith. In any case, it is important for you to take initiative in nurturing your own spiritual life.

7. The seminary community

Those who have not attended seminary sometimes idealize the community they expect to find there. You may assume that since most of the people enrolled in seminary are preparing for ministry and are serious about the church, this must be the ideal community for which every church wishes. You will be disappointed. The same irritating cast of characters that you find in your home church will be present in the seminary community. If you have the same difficulties with people in the seminary community that you have in your home church, you have a wonderful opportunity to ask if some of this may be about you rather than them.

Nevertheless, the community of people at a seminary and the ways in which they relate to one another are very important to your experience there. In the seminary community you will find a high percentage of people who are struggling with issues of vocation and faith. If these are your concerns, then you will find companions on the journey. Many times the informal conversations you have outside of class will have as great an impact as the classroom work. These settings are also a good opportunity to explore your motivations and gifts for ministry.

In recent years, the percentage of students who live off campus and commute to school has increased. While seminaries have begun to accommodate this reality by such innovations as providing evening classes and commuter rooms for overnight stays, the programs and structures of most seminaries still assume a residential student model. Commuters have to take more initiative to gain the benefits of the seminary community. For example, if you plan to be a commuter, you may want to arrange your schedule so you can be on campus for chapel or other worship opportunities. Having meals on campus if they are offered or inviting other students to go out to eat together is a good way to make informal connections. Some commuters I have known have taken initiative to form study groups with other students just so they could make more connections outside of class.

V. How should I choose a seminary?

1. Theological perspective

Seminaries do have theological perspectives. Some of them promote diversity, others seek greater uniformity. Some are conservative, others are more liberal. If a particular theological perspective is important to you, you will need to gear your research on seminaries to finding out about that. The theological perspective of a seminary will not necessarily be obvious from the structure of the curriculum or even the titles of the courses. These may look much the same in seminaries that are really very different from each other theologically. "Introduction to the New Testament" at one seminary may involve critical analysis of the text sources to reveal their limited and even potentially harmful perspectives, while a course by the same name at another seminary may foster an un-critical acceptance of the same texts' inerrancy.

So how can you tell the difference? To begin with, seminary cata-logs usually contain a mission statement that will give you a general idea about how the school understands its purpose, though some of these state-ments are too general to be useful. Ask an admissions officer if there are any additional documents about the beliefs the school supports. Taking a list of the faculty members to a theological library and looking up each one's publications could give you an idea of the range of their interests and viewpoints. You could choose some books or articles to read for a more in-depth picture. Recent graduates can also be helpful. The best way to assess the theological environment of a school is to visit: sit in on classes, talk to faculty, and most important, talk to students.

The denominational affiliation of a seminary can sometimes tell you something about its orientation, but it is not a certain indicator. While denominational seminaries usually reflect the theological perspective of their denomination, some denominational seminaries can be quite diverse in the theological perspectives represented. There are several reasons for this. First, many denominations have a fairly wide range of theological diversity within them. This diversity will show up in their seminaries. Second, most denominational seminaries these days are seeking students from outside their denominations in order to augment enrollments. This means that they have to appeal to a wider variety of students, but also that your experience in the classroom will be more diverse than it might have been 20 years ago. A third reason for increased theological diversity in seminaries is the fact that those enrolling now are likely to have changed denominations at least once in their lives and so embody a kind of diversity or at least flexibility within themselves.

Finally, many students choose a seminary because it is the one closest to home. It may not be one that fits their own theological perspective most closely, but they have ties to family or job that do not allow them to move away to a seminary that might be more congenial. For them, location is more important than theology.

2. Denominational vs. interdenominational

Seminaries that are officially related to a single denomination are usually oriented toward preparing people for ministry in that denomination. Their requirements will be tailored to meet the specific requirements for ordination in their sponsoring church. Most of their faculty are likely to be drawn from that denomination. However, they may have many students who come from other traditions as well. All seminaries are more interdenominational than they used to be.

Whether you want to attend a denominational seminary will depend partly on what you need. Some churches require that you attend one of their own denominationally sponsored seminaries if you are seeking ordination. Others have a list of approved seminaries. If you plan to seek ordination, it is important to inquire about this with your pastor or denominational officials. If you are somewhat new to the denomination in which you are seeking ordination, you may want to attend a denominational seminary even if it is not required, in order to become more familiar with the flavor of the denomination. If, on the other hand, you have grown up always attending churches in the same denomination, an inter-denominational seminary may broaden your perspective.

3. Stand-alone seminaries vs. university-related divinity schools

Seminaries that are independent and rely primarily on their own faculty and library resources are generally called "stand-alone" seminaries, while those that are part of a larger university are called "university-related" or "divinity schools." Either can be related to a specific denomination or be multi-denominational. Stand-alone seminaries often have a more separate sense of community, while university-related divinity schools may blur their boundaries with the larger academic community. University-related divinity schools usually offer the opportunity to take courses in other schools and departments in the university and may even have joint degree programs with other departments. Similar resources are also available at seminaries that have developed cooperative relationships with other nearby seminaries or universities.

4. Location

The first consideration about location is whether you are free to move or need to find a seminary within commuting distance of where you live now. If you are limited to seminaries nearby, then your choices are obviously fewer. However, your range of choices may be broadened somewhat by the fact that many seminaries attempt to provide accommodations for long-distance commuters. In some seminaries, classes are clustered so that you can attend all of your classes on one or two days a week. These schools may also have commuter rooms that can be rented by the night so you can come and stay over for a night or two.

If you are mobile, you have the advantage of a wider selection of seminaries. However, the context is still important. Some seminaries are in the center of urban areas; others are in small towns or rural settings. Some are located in close proximity to other seminaries and colleges or universities; others are more separate. Some are in contexts that are ethnically diverse; others have a more homogeneous environment.

You have to ask yourself what sort of setting will be best for you, in terms of both support and challenge. Are the resources you need—such as field placements and other training settings for ministry available? If you have specific desires about where you will find employment after graduation, you should also take into account how your location during seminary will affect that.

5. Accreditation

Accreditation is the means by which seminaries and other kinds of schools are reviewed by their peers in comparable institutions against standards of quality and content. As of 1996, there were 196 seminaries in the United States and Canada that were fully accredited by the Association of Theological Schools (ATS). Accreditation by ATS means that a seminary has met the standards established by the member schools.

Many seminaries are also accredited by the regional accrediting agencies that evaluate other schools, colleges, and universities. This means that they have met a broader set of standards than those specific to theological schools and that their degrees may be more widely recognized in the larger academic community.

There are also many seminaries that are not accredited by these agencies. Some of these are recognized by their own denomination and do not choose to seek wider acknowledgment. However, some form of accreditation or recognition demonstrates that a seminary is recognized by a specific group of peers.

6. How to get information

a) Catalogs
Of course, catalogs and other printed information are the basic ways that seminaries present information about themselves. Calling or writing for a catalog is a good way to start your investigation. Read about the faculty, the degree requirements, the courses offered. You will usually find a mission statement or statement of doctrine in the catalog. After you have read through a school's catalog, you will be more prepared to ask questions of the admissions office.

b) The seminary admissions office

Every seminary has one or more staff members, usually a director or dean of admissions, assigned to provide information to prospective students. These people are usually well informed about the seminary and anxious to talk to you. Many seminaries have toll-free telephone numbers to encourage you to call. Some of them have e-mail addresses.

The admissions officers will be able to clarify and expand on the information you have found in the catalog. They will have information about deadlines, prerequisites, financial aid, housing, and current developments in the seminary. If some part of the application process is unclear or seems not to apply to you, ask here first.

Of course, these admissions officers are usually charged with the task of recruitment as well and so will try to present the seminary in the best light. However, most of them are smart enough to know that it is not in the school's best interest to recruit students who will be unhappy there. The admissions office is an excellent source of information but should not be your only one.

c) People with firsthand knowledge: pastors, professors, graduates, current students

While printed materials and conversations with the admissions office provide good basic information, they can make seminaries sound more alike than they really are. Talking with people who have firsthand experience will be the best way to learn about the flavor and spirit of a school. This is where you will find the subtle but important distinctions among the seminaries you are considering.

You can start with pastors or professors you know, but the best resources are people who have graduated fairly recently from the seminary, as well as current students. They will be candid in their evaluations and will have a clear sense of how their education is serving them. Use your best networking skills to find the right people. Ask each person you consult if there is someone else you should talk to.

d) Denominational resources

If you are planning to seek ordination, you should seek counsel from denominational officials and boards or committees of ordained ministry. They may have suggestions or even requirements about which seminary you should attend. They will often have printed materials about the seminaries of your particular denomination.

e) Campus visits

If at all possible, you should visit the campus of any seminary you are considering. This is the most important way to get information. You want to know how it feels to be on the campus and with the people who are there. Try to arrange your visit when classes are in session so you can sit in on a few. Talk to students and faculty. Ask about financial aid. Spend enough time to get a sense of whether this is a place where you would grow and thrive. Remember, you will spend a significant piece of your life in this setting. What matters most is not just the length of time but the fact that it is a time when you will grow and change significantly. You want to be in an environment that both challenges and supports you in the ways you determine are important.

f) Internet resources

Many seminaries have websites and e-mail addresses. If you have access to the World Wide Web, this will be a quick way to gather some initial information and in some cases request catalogs and applications. The Association of Theological Schools maintains a list of accredited seminaries and their internet addresses at: http://www.ats.edu/members/alpha.htm.

VI. What about the logistics?

1. Getting ordained

Churches ordain people, seminaries don't. If you want to be ordained and are not solidly connected with a denomination, finding a church is your first priority. Some people think seminary is like law school and plan to finish school, then put out their résumés to various denominations. It doesn't work that way. For a church or denomination to consider ordaining you, it has to have some history with you, has to get to know you. It will want to have seen you as an active member and even a leader before recommending you for ordination.

If you are even entertaining the thought of ordained ministry, exploring your denomination's ordination process should be one of your first steps. This may influence your choice of a seminary. Further, in many denominations the various interviews and processes that lead to ordination may take as long as or longer than completing the M.Div. degree. It is important to start early.

The best place to start is with your own pastor. She or he will usually know what the first steps are and may be able to provide you with some important mentoring through the process. Some ministers may not be entirely clear on the process and may refer you to someone in the denomination who works with the ordination procedure. Don't be afraid to talk to lots of people. Take initiative in understanding the process and make sure you start and stay on track.

Ordination is not guaranteed just because you graduate from seminary. It is very possible that you could graduate from seminary with a stellar academic record and still not be approved by your denomination for ordination. Most denominational ordination processes provide many opportunities along the way for you to receive feedback on how you are doing and what your chances are. Taking this information into account and making the necessary adjustments can save you from a painful shock at the end of seminary.

2. Applying to seminary

a) Prerequisites
In general, the degrees offered by seminaries are at the graduate level and require a bachelor's degree for admission. A strong background in the liberal arts and social sciences is the best preparation, but a bachelor's degree in other fields may be adequate.

However, even if you lack an undergraduate degree, you should not hesitate to talk to an admissions officer about your options. Some seminaries have special programs for people without undergraduate degrees. Sometimes older students who have some undergraduate work and significant leadership experience in the church can enroll under special circumstances. It's always worth asking.

When you get serious about applying, be sure to ask if there are any other prerequisites besides your undergraduate transcripts. Some seminaries require the Graduate Record Examination or other testing and you may need to allow time for those results to reach the seminary before its deadlines.

b) Deadlines
Many seminaries accept applications on a "rolling" basis, meaning that they accept and review applications throughout the year and may be willing to admit new students right up to the time of registration for a new term. Others have firm deadlines that are well in advance of enrollment. In either case, applying early increases your chances of success. While you have control over the application parts that you write, people whom you ask to write letters of recommendation may be slow. Meeting a deadline usually means having all of one's materials in to the school. It is only common courtesy to give those people writing recommendations time to fit this favor into their schedules. On the other hand, even your best friend sometimes needs reminding. Take responsibility for seeing that all of your materials are in before the deadline.

God is notorious for ignoring the application deadlines. It's June when you hear the call to attend seminary in the fall, but the deadline for application was March 1. Why didn't God call in January? What do you do? Don't give up. Start by asking someone in the admissions office if there is any way you can start in the fall. Some seminaries are relatively flexible in their application deadlines. Of course, if they tell you that there is no possibility of applying at this point, there is no advantage in pressing the issue and making a pest of yourself. You want these people to be your allies. If the deadline for application to degree programs has passed, it may still be possible for you to begin as a nondegree student and add those credits to your degree when you are admitted later on. Again, it doesn't hurt to ask.

3. Paying for it

Whether you belong in seminary at this moment in your life is a financial question as well as a vocational question. You cannot just assume that because you are called to ministry and want to go to seminary, everything will be taken care of for you. (Some people think that way, believe it or not.) While money is not primary in our lives, San Francisco State University professor Jacob Needleman, in his book *Money and the Meaning of Life,* says, "...if we do not give sufficient attention to what is secondary in life, then, sooner or later, what is secondary will take all our attention and leave us no energy or time to pursue what is most essential."[1] I am amazed at the sacrifices people make to come to seminary when they feel called. I am usually inspired by them, but sometimes they worry me. Good stewardship involves wise financial planning.

a) How much does it cost?
Unless you are independently wealthy, you will need to pay careful attention to juggling the many factors affecting total seminary costs. Careful planning pays off in your ability to concentrate on your education.

While seminaries vary fairly widely in their actual tuition charges, that is not always an accurate indication of which will cost you more. The seminary with the higher tuition may also award more financial aid. You need to look at the bottom line. Usually a seminary's financial aid office can give you an estimate of expenses and potential financial aid before you apply. This can help you with your advance planning before you finally nail it down by actually applying. Some denominational seminaries even give free tuition to those who have been endorsed for ministry by their own denomination. Check it out.

b) Where can I find support?

Most denominations have some scholarships to support seminary students. You may need to apply for these separately and to a different source (probably a denominational office) from your seminary financial-aid application. Denominational scholarship programs usually require that you apply many months in advance of the term for which the award will be made. Investigate this procedure early. On the other hand, after the first round of awards has been made, there is sometimes still money available. It never hurts to ask. Some denominational funds come from the national level, while others may be administered by the local conference or synod. You will need to do some research. Denominations also may have specific scholarships for racial ethnic minorities, women, or other underrepresented categories. In almost all cases, they award the largest amount of money to those preparing for parish ministry.

All seminaries have some program of financial aid. It may include tuition discounts, scholarships, grants, work-study, field-education placements, or loans. You should find out early how to apply for any available aid. Where aid is based on need, you will have to fill out statements on your own financial situation. Often this requires completing your income tax early in the year (not a bad thing to do anyway). Other scholarships consider your prior academic record, your leadership experience, your promise for ministry, or your plans to enter a specific ministry. Some local congregations provide financial support to their members.

I want to offer a special word about loans. Student loans are playing an increasingly significant role in financing seminary education. While some churches and seminaries have their own loan programs, most of these loans come from the same federal student loan programs used by undergraduate students. In recent years these loans have become available to more people in greater amounts. My experience, which is confirmed in conversations with colleagues, is that while most students use good judgment in borrowing, there are some who borrow too much. Some even depend on credit cards and other consumer debt to cover education costs. You must exercise extreme caution here. Income from any of the professions normally issuing from a seminary education will be quite modest. Large loan payments could distract you from your chosen work or even require you to quit in favor of work that allows you to repay your loans. Borrow prudently.

c) Can I keep my job?

Good question—in fact, not a bad idea. More and more people are attending seminary this way. If you are well-established in a job, making decent money, and not totally fed up with it, you are probably financially better off than you would be washing dishes in the seminary dining hall. It's sort of the "bird in the hand" principle. Of course, the answer really depends on how well you can match your work schedule with that of the seminary. Will your current employer offer you a part-time or flexible schedule? Some people continue to work full-time while in seminary. Most don't find that possible. If you need to work full-time, you may need to attend seminary part-time.

On the other hand, some find it preferable to take a job on campus even though the pay is lower, because it is convenient and helps one feel more a part of the community. The field-education placements required of most M.Div. students often carry a modest stipend. Sometimes it is possible to extend these placements beyond the required year.

d) Is this the right time?

When you begin to feel certain that you belong in seminary, you will probably also feel an urgency to get started. You are not unusual if you want to start right now whether it's the middle of the summer or Christmas vacation. Other factors may intervene—such as money or your spouse's career or your children's education. You may need to learn to live patiently with your decision until the time is right to start.

In the meantime, you may be able to begin by taking a course or two at a nearby seminary or even some courses in religious studies at a college or university. If you decide to do that, it's worth checking with the seminary you want to attend to see if those courses will count toward your degree when you eventually enroll. There is sometimes an "elapsed time" rule stipulating that credit can be given only for courses taken within a certain time period. Usually the registrar or the dean can answer these questions.

If you have to wait to attend seminary, there may also be ways you can be involved in ministry or work that will inform your choices and preparation. Look for places to volunteer in either your church or a community agency. This experience will provide valuable material for reflection when you are engaged in academic work later on and may also strengthen your application to the degree program.

4. Part-time or full-time?

Increasingly, people are attending seminary part-time, usually for financial reasons. Until recently, seminaries were organized totally for the full-time student, but in recent years most have shifted schedules and requirements to accommodate part-time students. The obvious advantage of attending part-time is that you can earn money to support your education and perhaps decrease your dependence on loans. If your work is in a related area, it may also provide a nice complement to your study.

On the other hand, there are strong advantages to enrolling full-time if you can swing it. Most schools still organize their courses in a sequence that is more tailored to the full-time student. Part-time students often find themselves taking courses out of order and even putting off basic requirements until later in their program. Part-time students also miss out on many of the benefits of the informal community life. For many, this is just as important as the classroom experience. You are probably in seminary to prepare for work in which your identity as a person is as important as the knowledge you have absorbed. Thus this informal community environment is especially important.

5. Living on campus or commuting?

In many respects, the same issues apply here as to the question of enrolling full-time or part-time. Commuting may allow you to stay in your current home or close to your job, but living on campus allows you to participate more fully in the seminary community. Living on campus may be cheaper, too; most seminary housing is subsidized to some degree. Some seminaries, however, have little housing and are located where off-campus housing is scarce or expensive. You'll need to inquire and make your own calculations.

If you have a family, you will also want to consider the advantages and disadvantages for them. Parish ministry places particular stresses on the pastor's family, so in some respects the whole family needs to be preparing. Living in close proximity with others who are preparing for similar ministries offers opportunities for sharing and common experience for your family as well as for you.

6. Family considerations

Your decision to attend seminary will have a significant impact on the other members of your household. How supportive is your spouse or partner of this change? What economic effect will this have on the whole family? Will your children have to change schools? What will their experience be? All of these questions should be discussed carefully with everyone involved. Some people find it helpful to have a few sessions with a family counselor in order to make sure everyone's concerns have been heard.

After you have begun seminary, you will want to be sure that your spouse or partner does not feel completely left out. This is an exciting time in your life. You will be encountering new ideas and discussing them with new and interesting colleagues. For this reason it is important to pay special attention to personal relationships during these times. Most seminaries provide for spouses and partners to be involved and to audit a few courses if they wish. This is a good idea. At the very least, any couple needs to be conscious of nurturing the relationship in a time when one partner is growing rapidly.

a) Spouse/partner's employment

There are two considerations here. The first is that your spouse or partner may have a job he or she likes and giving it up would be a great sacrifice. How will you handle this? If you are moving to a new community, will there be opportunities for a similar job? If pursuing a particular profession is important to your spouse or partner, then he or she may want to have a job assured before you enroll in seminary.

Second, many seminary students could not afford to attend school without the income of a working spouse. This may be a reversal of roles in the family and can be a source of conflict. If you have been the main financial support for the family, but are now dependent on your spouse's income, you may find that a source of your sense of self-worth has been removed. On the other hand, if you are enjoying the freedom and new adventure of school while your spouse is feeling the drudgery of nine to five, there is also room for resentments to arise. There may be shifts in the division of responsibilities for housework and childcare to be negotiated. All of these situations can put stress on your relationship, but they can also be opportunities for growth if both of you pay attention to your feelings and stay in conversation.

b) Children's schools
Moves to new schools can disrupt children's lives and sense of well-being. You will want to learn as much as you can about the schools they will be attending while you are in seminary. Perhaps an advance visit will be possible. Ask the seminary for the names of other students with children similar in age to yours. Ask them about the schools and perhaps arrange an opportunity for your children to meet theirs.

Many children are fascinated by the fact that Mom or Dad will have homework, too. However, this may get old pretty quickly when they find out that it also means Mom or Dad has less time for them. It is easy to neglect children's needs in the excitement of a change or move, when they may actually need more attention than usual.

7. Acting on faith (within reason)

There comes a time when you have thought through every aspect and issue that you can identify. Then you have to step forward on faith. Sometimes, despite your best efforts, you are not able to see beyond the next step. The only way to do so is to take it. We are not talking about "blind" faith here. We are talking about engaging in all the best research, dialogue, and thinking that you can, then stepping forward on faith.

When you finally decide to take the next step, flexibility is important. Sometimes people treat the decision to go to seminary with so much awe and heaviness that they assume it is set in concrete. It isn't. It is perfectly honorable to change your mind if you find that the direction you have chosen is not working for you.

VII. Will I get a job?

Even morticians and tax collectors are subject to the laws of supply and demand. Changing circumstances, regional differences, your own gifts, your willingness to move, your economic needs all affect your relation to the job market. Your most reliable information will come from talking to people in the kinds of work and locations that interest you. The following is a description of some general trends and particular strategies that may help you in your own investigation.

1. Parish ministry

Most mainline Protestant denominations have predicted a shortage of pastors due to rising numbers of retirements during the 1990s by pastors who entered ministry during the 1950s and '60s. So far this shortage has not been as great as was expected. Some ministers have chosen to work past the age of 65. Some who were ordained but not serving churches have returned to the parish. However, you can expect the rate of retirements to continue rising, both because of the age of long-term clergy and the increasing number of second-career persons entering ministry at a later age. The fact that people are, in general, living longer has led to a growing pool of retired clergy, often putting stress on denominational budgets that must pay for underfunded pensions. This has even led to some discussions in ordaining bodies of the possibility of placing some limits on the number of people ordained.

Declining membership in mainline denominations will also have a limiting effect on opportunities as some churches close and others can afford only a part-time pastor. Most denominations are considering alternative ways of serving smaller churches such as using lay pastors or yoking two or more churches together. If you are considering parish ministry, you may want to ask yourself if you are willing to serve in a part-time position or in more than one church.

The reality of declining memberships raises another issue for persons considering parish ministry: how will you respond to a placement in a congregation that has declined in numbers? Are you a person who can bring energy and hope to such a situation? Will you see your role as simply presiding over further decline? Will you become discouraged by small or no gains?

For some, a part-time position is a positive prospect. If you have a working spouse or another part-time job, part-time parish ministry can be a satisfying life, but you should not enter such a position without a clear plan for how to contain this part-time work. The needs of ministry are always unlimited and can expand to whatever time you give them. A clear agreement with the congregation, especially one accustomed to a full-time pastor, is essential. Are you a person who can say "no" with grace and conviction?

a) Prospects for women

There have always been women in seminaries, but traditionally they were preparing for specialized ministries, especially in Christian education. Over the past 25 years or so, there has been a dramatic increase in the number of women in M.Div. programs and entering parish ministry. In 1972 there were 1,077 women in M.Div. and comparable professional degree programs enrolled in seminaries accredited by the ATS. That was 4.7 percent of the total.[1] In 1996 there were 7,968 women enrolled in M.Div. programs or 28.6 percent of the total.[2] In fact, there are currently a number of seminaries that have more than two-thirds women in their M.Div. programs.

Progressive denominations and seminaries have welcomed these women and affirmed their ministries. More conservative congregations, denominations, and seminaries have been slower to accept them. While acceptance of women in pastoral ministry is clearly increasing, a woman considering parish ministry should be prepared for the likelihood that it will still be more difficult to find a position than for her male classmates. Researcher Patricia M. Y. Chang has also shown that the average salary for women in parish ministry is substantially lower than for men. She says, "In some of the clearest evidence of discrimination, analysis of earnings differentials show that women clergy earn roughly 9 percent less than their male counterparts even after adjusting for age, experience, education, denomination, type of clergy position, size of congregation, and ideological conservativism."[3] The proportion of women who are pastors of large multi-staff congregations is also smaller. Chang says that women "...are more likely than men to end up in positions which pay less, have lower levels of benefits, less job security, and fewer opportunities for 'upward mobility' into larger churches with greater responsibilities."[4] Not surprisingly, a recent study showed that women leave the ministry at a higher rate than men, suggesting a higher level of dissatisfaction among women.[5]

On the other hand, when you consider the relatively recent entrance of large numbers of women into parish ministry, their acceptance has been remarkably fast. I feel certain this trend will continue. You can best obtain a reliable picture of the situation in your own denomination by consulting several female pastors and asking them about their experience. In addition to learning about your job prospects, you may also learn some strategies to enhance your chances.

b) Prospects for people of color

If you are a member of a racial ethnic minority, your situation will vary greatly from one denomination to another. If you belong to a denomination comprised primarily of people of your own ethnicity, then race is obviously no barrier. On the other hand, if you are a racial ethnic member of a predominantly white denomination, your situation is more complex. You need to do some research to learn whether you might be limited to churches of your own ethnicity, or if there are many churches in your denomination that are open to having a pastor of a race different from their own. If you are limited to serving certain churches, you need to ask how many there are in this denomination that will be open to you. If you discover there is a greater openness, you still have to also ask yourself how you feel about pastoring a church of a different ethnicity from yours.

Again, the best resource for information will be people of your own racial ethnic group. You will learn from them more accurate information about the real situation than you will from denominational policies and official statements. Unfortunately, the reality often does not measure up to the church's good intentions.

c) Prospects for lesbians and gay men

If you are gay, lesbian, or bisexual, you are undoubtedly aware of the recent debates raging in most mainline denominations over whether to ordain "self-avowed, practicing" homosexuals. There are deep divisions in all denominations over this issue—whatever their decision has been over the ordination of homosexuals. In those denominations that have taken a stand to prohibit ordination of gay and lesbian ministers, there are still substantial numbers of persons who favor it. On the other hand, those denominations that permit ordination of homosexuals may have difficulty placing them because individual congregations are more conservative.

As a gay, lesbian, or bisexual person, you need to look carefully at your prospects. If your own denomination is not supportive of your ordination, you may be faced with finding another. Even in those denominations that are willing to ordain you, you need to ask whether gay and lesbian seminary graduates are finding jobs. The Metropolitan Community Church is a denomination made up primarily of gay and lesbian members and is clearly open to your ministry. Although it is growing, it is still small (approximately 300 churches worldwide) and therefore has a relatively small number of pastoral positions available. One way you may have more chance of finding a position is if you are willing to work on starting a new congregation of the denomination in a community where there is not one. This is very hard work and will undoubtedly start out part-time and require you to have another job to support yourself.

As with women in ministry, openness to gay and lesbian ministers is increasing, but much more slowly. You have to ask yourself whether you are cut out for being a pioneer and how you will deal with the battles you may have to undertake. While some lesbians and gay men have chosen to keep their sexual orientation closeted in order to remain in ministry, I cannot honestly recommend this route for someone starting out. The stress on your own integrity and personhood is too great.

d) Prospects for people with disabilities

In recent years the church has become increasingly open to the gifts of persons with disabilities. As congregations have become aware of the need to make their buildings and programs more accessible to participants with disabilities, they have also become more open to differently-abled pastors. As might be expected, some congregations are more receptive than others, but there are many receiving leadership from people with hearing impairment, mobility limitations, blindness, and a host of other disabilities. My oldest and best friend is almost totally deaf and is the pastor of a large United Methodist church in California. His church recognizes his gifts and willingly makes the necessary adjustments. Another friend who is legally blind serves a church in Washington with effectiveness and creativity that is a blessing to her congregation. In many respects, persons with disabilities have a head start in understanding the needs and struggles of their parishioners.

If you have a disability that affects the way in which you can exercise ministry, you will certainly have to carefully assess the impact that will have on your effectiveness. You will also have to be prepared for resistance from those unaccustomed to adjusting to the special needs of their pastor. You will not automatically be evaluated on the basis of your gifts rather than your limitations. You will have to be willing to take on the task of educating your congregation to your special needs. Of course, if you have had this disability for any length of time, you already know that that is a task you undertake everywhere you go.

The good news is that most denominations have adopted policies of non-discrimination and have begun to develop resources to assist the church in receiving the gifts of those with disabilities.

e) Prospects for second-career people

Twenty-five years ago, most people entered seminary directly from college at the age of 21 or 22. Today the average age at some seminaries is pushing 40. Part of this age increase results from the enrollment of women who would have gone to seminary earlier if it had been acceptable. But there are also increasing numbers of men entering ministry in mid-life. While at the denominational level there has been some resistance to these older candidates, especially by those concerned about health care and pensions, congregations have for the most part been quick to realize the advantages of a new minister with maturity and life experience. All in all, second-career people have very good prospects for pastoral placements upon seminary graduation.

f) Opportunities for advancement

You may want to think carefully about your own gifts as well as your image of parish ministry in relation to the size of congregation you might find yourself serving. On the one hand, you might serve a small church where ministry is primarily a matter of the pastor's relationship to the individual members. This is a significantly different job from serving a larger church where ministry is carried out through programs and the pastor has more of an administrative role. If your primary experience of the church has been in the latter sort, you may find yourself surprised by the very different experience in a small church.

While our image of advancement tends to involve moving from a smaller church to a larger church, you may find your gifts and interests more related to one or the other. If you "do the math" in most any area of the country, you will find that there are not enough large churches to "reward" all of the people serving small churches. Many people spend their entire careers serving smaller churches and find it very satisfying. However, if your image of advancement is "bigger is better," you should try to have an accurate picture of the real possibilities.

2. Academic careers

If you are considering seminary in preparation for an academic career, then you will most likely be planning to continue on to a Ph.D. program after your master's degree. This is a big commitment of time and money. You should look carefully at the difficulties of finding a teaching job once you have completed all this education. While there have been some forecasts of large numbers of retirements in the coming decade, religion and religious studies departments have been among the first to be cut as funding for higher education has decreased.

In order to increase your chances of finding a teaching position in a college, avoid specializing too narrowly so that you will be prepared to teach a wide variety of subjects within a religious studies department or even in the wider humanities. You might also consider whether you are willing to take on an administrative job in higher education—in student services, for example. Sometimes these come with part-time teaching responsibilities. Flexibility will make you more employable.

There is also significant competition for positions in seminary teaching. Pastoral experience in addition to your doctoral work will enhance your chances here. If you are planning to be ordained, some denominations require two or three years in parish ministry prior to ordination even if you plan on some other ministry. This may mean spending a few years in the parish before going on to doctoral work. Many seminaries are consciously trying to increase the diversity of their faculties, which has led to a relatively high demand for the best ethnically diverse faculty.

3. Other forms of ministry

There are as many possible forms of ministry as there are people and needs in the world. I will mention only the most common.

a) Chaplaincy
A chaplain is ordinarily an ordained pastor assigned to ministry in an institution such as a college, hospital, prison, or the military, although there are some non-ordained people in these positions as well. As a chaplain, you are different from a parish minister in that you do not have a specific congregation to whom you are accountable. Rather, you provide pastoral services to one group of people (say patients or students) while you are accountable to another (say a denomination or the administration of the institution). In addition to their general theological education, most chaplains have some sort of specialized training in working with the specific population they serve. The nature of this training varies from institution to institution as well as from one location to another. If you are drawn toward chaplaincy, query people who are in the kind of position that interests you, talk to the administrators in charge of hiring, and contact any relevant professional organizations.

Competition for positions in chaplaincy is generally very stiff. The pool of applicants for an open position often includes people with extensive experience in parish ministry as well as some with experience in the specific kind of job. Having done Clinical Pastoral Education (CPE) in a similar institution will improve your chances. You may also want to consider volunteering in a chaplaincy program to gain some experience. In general, however, it is somewhat difficult to find a chaplaincy position right out of seminary.

b) Pastoral Counseling
According to the American Association of Pastoral Counselors (A.A.P.C.), "Pastoral Counselors are ministers or persons endorsed by a religious faith group who are also mental health professionals. They have received

specialized graduate training in both religion and the behavioral sciences and practice the integrated discipline of pastoral counseling."[6] A pastoral counselor is endorsed as a minister in good standing in a recognized religious body and has a continuing responsible relationship with a local community of faith.

If you were licensed by the state as a psychotherapist or some other form of counselor, then your primary accountability would be to a state board. Pastoral counselors are not licensed by the state, so they are accountable to their own faith community and the American Association of Pastoral Counselors. This ministry, like all others, is grounded in community. Members of the A.A.P.C. generally have B.A. and M.Div. degrees from accredited schools as well as specialized classes and supervised practice in pastoral counseling.

Pastoral counseling is an essential part of many forms of ministry, so many seek this training without intending to be full-time pastoral counselors. Before you embark upon seminary training with the intention of becoming a pastoral counselor, you should do two things. First, contact the A.A.P.C.[7] for an outline of their specific membership requirements as well as a list of approved training programs. Second, seek out some people who are working in the area of pastoral counseling and talk with them about the availability of jobs. You may have some difficulty finding many such persons in your area, which is more likely due to the scarcity of positions than to a shortage of pastoral counselors. If you do decide to pursue this specialized form of ministry, be prepared to be creative and entrepreneurial about finding or creating a place for yourself.

c) Professional lay ministry in the church

Traditionally, the most common areas of professional lay ministry are in the areas of education, youth ministry, and music. However, churches also hire trained laypeople as church administrators, volunteer coordinators, parish nurses, community outreach workers, parish visitors, childcare workers, senior citizen program directors, and for an ever-increasing range of new ministries. Obviously, these positions are much more prevalent in large churches that can support a multiple and diverse staff. However, you may also be able to create a job for yourself by working part-time at more than one church. Finding the right position in lay ministry requires initiative and imagination.

d) Nonprofit organizations

Increasingly, seminary graduates are finding exciting work in nonprofit community programs. These jobs are often demanding and may not be highly paid. They are likely to depend on "soft money" that can disappear if the foundation or government grant does not come through that year. On the other hand, these jobs offer wonderful opportunities for making a difference in the community and providing services for people who are often poorly served.

It is not possible to generalize about the nature of these jobs. Each one is different. Before you take a specific job you should investigate how secure the funding is for this position and measure that over against your own tolerance for risk. You want to be as clear as possible about the specific work you will be doing. Sometimes the job descriptions overstate the amount of time you will spend serving clients and underestimate how much of the job is actually administration and fundraising. Don't forget, however, that administration and fundraising are also ministries.

e) Finding/creating that one-of-a-kind job

Many people find their way to seminary as part of their pursuit of some very particular vision of a call that does not fit any job that exists. Some of these people end up just where they hoped to be; others leave more lost than when they began. The difference lies in two factors. The first is how connected their vision is to community. Those who pursue a purely individual vision and who are unwilling to be accountable to others in this quest usually don't find their place. It's still surprising to me how many people come to talk to me about seminary and say that they would like to be a minister, but can't stand the idea of having to relate to a congregation that may have ideas different than their own. If your vision of a particular ministry is grounded in the needs of a community, you have a good chance of finding or creating a place for yourself.

The second factor that will influence your success in finding that one-of-a-kind job is your initiative. There are those who operate on the assumption that such a job should be somehow created and handed to them. While there is an element of grace in any successful job search, those who take initiative and responsibility, those who have tenacity and determination, are more likely to find their place than those who wait for God or the church to provide.

4. Taking initiative

Because you have a sense of calling and are ready to make personal sacrifices in order to serve, you may feel that you should not really have to go looking for a job. Someone should be waiting to offer one to you. You are not alone if you feel that way. However, that is not the way it works, and I would recommend that you not waste any precious energy feeling resentful about it. In fact, I would go so far as to say that the seminary graduates who make the greatest contributions and who find their work most satisfying are those who take the strongest initiative in finding the best place to do the work to which they have been called. Don't wait for the work to come to you. Start early and take charge of the search.

VIII. Do I belong in seminary?

By now I hope you are aware that there are lots of different reasons for going to seminary. Malcolm Warford says,

> ...seminaries are no longer places simply for the education of clergy; instead, they are centers of theological education for all Christians and our companions along the way. This means there should be a radical openness to the diversity of gifts and the forms of ministry to which Christ calls us. Some require ordination, most do not, but all of them demand knowledge of the gospel and theological traditions that establish our believing in practices of faith that embody our call to responsibility.[1]

So how will you decide if seminary is the place for you at this moment in your life?

1. The many sides of discernment

Don't base your decision on one factor or experience alone. There are many sides of this question to consider: your own sense of call, the church's confirmation, your family situation, financial realities, your own gifts and abilities, the possibility of getting a job, and probably several others you can think of. While you don't want to let the complexity of the decision immobilize you, you do want to make this decision with all the relevant information you can gather. There are also many sources of help in making your decision. Draw on as many of them as you can. Pastors, friends, family, seminary students, vocational counselors, seminary admissions officers, denominational officials, and even financial advisors may have something to add to your decision.

You may have a dramatic and life-changing experience and assume that it decides everything. It is wonderful to have such a moving experience, but you should also look to other sources for confirmation. The need for testing is especially vital if you have gone through a traumatic event that has shaken the foundations of your life. It is not uncommon for people to consider seminary after a divorce or the death of a loved one or the failure of a business. These are important watershed events in your life, but they are also times when you are vulnerable to making decisions that are not carefully considered. So draw on as many resources for discernment as you can. I have mentioned some of these resources in earlier parts of this book, but I return to them now to help you make the best decision you can.

2. Worship, Bible study, journaling, and prayer

Your own spiritual practices and resources are at the foundation of whatever you do, so use them intentionally as you make this decision. Carry the vocational question with you into whatever settings of spiritual practice you have. You may find that corporate worship speaks to you more directly than usual if you come with an open spirit. If that is true for you, you might want to seek out additional times and opportunities for worship.

Studying the Bible not only provides a context for life decisions, it also provides myriad examples of people responding to God's call. Some of those situations may speak to you in a particular way. On the other hand, don't be intimidated by dramatic stories that seem beyond your experience. Everyone's call is different. The Bible is wonderfully diverse. Perhaps you will be able to find one or two other people to do this Bible study with you.

Keeping a journal is another way of being open to God's guidance. Set aside a time simply to write down whatever comes to you about this decision. Don't censor your thoughts; you won't have to show this to anyone. You will be amazed what you find yourself saying. One of the benefits of keeping a journal is that you can look back and discover that certain themes come up repeatedly over time. You may discover a sense of direction in the guidance you receive.

Set aside time daily to put yourself in a listening mode. If you have a regular practice of prayer or meditation, focus it on this decision. If you don't have a regular spiritual practice, this is a good time to try it out. Don't start out by setting your sights too high or being too self-critical. The easiest way to start is to find a time in the day to designate as little as ten minutes when you can gently set aside all the other worries and tasks of your life and simply listen to the sound of your own breath. Thoughts will naturally arise; notice them and let them go. Remember that God loves you and will take care of holding other things together while you stop and listen for ten minutes.

3. Conferences and retreats

Most denominations have a more or less structured discernment process for those who are considering ordained ministry. The early phases of this process may be helpful to you. Sometimes they have conferences or retreats that are specifically designed for people who are in the process of making vocational decisions. In addition to some structured leadership, you will find at such events support and guidance from other participants who are on similar journeys.

Most seminaries sponsor events for people who are considering attending. These will probably be more focused on the resources and strengths of the particular seminary, but they can give you a sense of what being there will be like. Many of them also provide leadership in the process of vocational discernment. Here again, being with people who are in the process of making the same decision is a great resource. Call the admissions office of any seminary you are considering and ask if they have such an event.

4. People who can help

Ultimately, you must take responsibility for your own decision. No one can make it for you. You are also responsible for gathering and checking all of the information you need. An important part of making a responsible decision is to seek out the people who can help. Who can help you? Perhaps the most important answer to this question is that you need a variety of perspectives, thus a variety of people. You need people who will be supportive of you, people who know you well, people who are familiar with the field of ministry you plan to enter, people who will be brutally honest with you about your gifts and prospects, people who are familiar with the resources of seminaries. One person cannot be all of these things to you. Local congregations are notoriously prone to being supportive of anyone who expresses a desire to enter ministry and having a hard time saying "no" to one of their own. You want support, but you also want honesty.

Your pastor is the most accessible resource for guidance about seminary and ministry. Ask him or her specifically to spend time with you exploring your decision. Some pastors are better at this than others. (They aren't perfect, you know.) If you feel that your concerns are not being heard accurately or if your pastor seems simply to project his or her own experience onto your situation, you may have to be a little assertive in making yourself clear. In a large church there may be other ministers on the staff who are more helpful to you. Perhaps there is another pastor in a neighboring church who can work with you. Some pastors are better informed about denominational processes and seminary options than others. So be sure to double check with other resources.

Perhaps you will want to find a mentor. In *The Odyssey* Ulysses asked a wise man named "Mentor" to care for his son, Telemachus, while Ulysses was off at the Trojan war. Mentor not only taught Telemachus academic subjects, but also helped him grow into being a man in the world. That story is where we get the word "mentor." You will need different kinds of mentors at different times in your life. Mostly they are people who have traveled the road ahead of you. They are persons who can give you advice, offer both challenge and support, be role models. Sometimes mentoring relationships are informal and brief, but it is important to have more structured mentoring relationships for times of important growth in your life. You can take initiative to set up such a relationship with someone you respect.

If you are in a formal exploration process with a denomination, it is likely an assigned mentor will guide you. This is an important resource, but don't be afraid to seek out others if this person doesn't meet your needs. Find a compatible person who understands your goals, with whom you relate easily, and who is willing to spend significant time with you.

The various committees and steps you have to go through on the way to ordination have a dual, and sometimes confused, purpose. On the one hand, they are designed to nurture and mentor those on their way to ordination. On the other, they are the "gate-keepers" assigned to make sure that those ordained are truly called and qualified. No person or committee handles this perfectly; most do their best. The result, however, is that sometimes you feel supported and other times you may feel under attack. The goal for everyone in this process, including you, is to be sure the ministry you are pursuing is right for you. The ordination process will help you sharpen the focus of your vocation. You will become more articulate about your call, but you may also find a more specialized direction than you had at the beginning. As noted earlier, any call to ministry is not just a personal matter. Examination by the various committees leading to ordination are how the church exercises its responsibility to confirm your call. It is a means of testing as well as a means of support.

Friends and family know and love you and are an essential support in this process. But these people who know you best also have a personal stake in this decision. Your friends have a familiar image of you that may have to change. Your family will be affected and may not yet be ready for what would be required of them. It may be that your friends and family are already urging you in this direction or it may be that it scares them. In any case, these people see you up close and personal and should have an intimate and ongoing role in your decision. They are the ones who love you most and care most about your well-being.

Seminary admissions officers have a different kind of stake in your decision. They may even have an admissions quota to fill. However, if they are wise, they know that recruiting you to their seminary when it is the wrong place for you does neither you nor the seminary a favor. These people have a lot of specific information that you can use. They understand the details of the degree programs in their seminary, are familiar with the faculty, and know the student body. They can answer questions about finances and scholarships. They can direct you to resources in your denomination as well. Don't be shy about calling them on their 800 number any time you think of another question. That's what they are paid for.

You can also ask them about other seminaries. Who are their competitors? What should you consider in choosing among seminaries? Again, the best admissions people will have a collegial relationship with their counterparts in other seminaries and will be concerned that you make a good decision.

Talk to students. You can get the most raw and unmediated perspective on what seminary is like from those who are currently in the midst of it. Most of them are not neutral. They either hate it or love it. Sometimes their feelings are related to the particular time of the semester and the proximity of final papers. By talking to a variety of students, you can get a sense of whether this particular seminary is the right place for you, while also enriching your understanding of seminary in general. Most students, even those employed by the admissions office, are willing to be pretty honest about their experience. Ask them how they decided to go to seminary.

If you don't know any seminary students, ask the admissions office to connect you with some who would be willing to talk with you. Ask if there is someone with a similar background and similar interests to yours. You can do this by telephone or in person. If you can visit a seminary, hang out in the dining hall or other places where students gather and strike up a conversation. Most are more than willing to talk about their experience.

5. Trying on your call

Being the chair of a committee or the leader of a ministry in your local congregation gives you an opportunity to experience your gifts in the context of community. Being a lay reader or preacher in worship is an opportunity to develop skills essential to ministry. Teaching a Sunday school or Bible study class is a way of testing your teaching gifts. Many denominations require this kind of experience as a prerequisite to the first steps in the ordination process.

You may find that your gifts are used adequately as a layperson in the church and decide that you are really called to continue in your current work while increasing the level of volunteer work you do. This would not necessarily mean you would not decide to attend seminary. Some choose to seek further training without changing their occupations.

Short-term opportunities such as work camps, camp counseling, and mission internships are available in most churches. They are an opportunity to immerse yourself more fully in contexts of ministry. You may even want to take on a year-long internship in this testing process.

6. Testing the seminary waters

Visiting a seminary is the best thing you can do. I learned this from my
sons when they were choosing colleges. I wanted to study the catalogs to
learn about the curriculum and the faculty. They wanted to walk around
the campus and see how it felt to be there. They were mostly right. You
are going to spend two or three years of your life living in this place.
You need to feel that it is an environment in which you can grow and
thrive.

Ask to sit in on a few classes in order to get a sense of the teaching
styles and the perspectives of the faculty. Spend time in the informal
environments of the seminary—the library, the cafeteria, the coffee shop
–and learn what the students are like. Surveys of seminary students indi-
cate that fellow students are nearly as important as faculty in what they
learned in seminary. Walk or drive around the neighboring community.
Is this a place you want to live?

You can take this testing a step further by actually enrolling in a
seminary. Most seminaries will allow you to take at least a course or two
without being enrolled in a degree program. If there is a seminary within
commuting distance of where you live, this can give you a taste of the
real thing. Be sure to ask if the credit you receive for these courses can
be applied to a degree later on. If you are thinking of going to a different
seminary for your degree program, you may want to check with that one
to see if it will accept this credit.

Many seminaries actually have one-year programs designed for
people who want to explore seminary education. In most cases, these
courses will apply to other degree programs if you decide to go on. Even
if you do not go on for another degree, you own education and faith will
be enhanced by this experience.

7. Taking the next step

You really can take only one step at a time. Sometimes it helps to realize
that whatever you decide to do is only the *next* step. This is a journey
you are on, not a final destination. Seminaries are notorious as places
where people change direction often. And even if you go through all the
considerations I have suggested in this book and decide against seminary,

you will probably find yourself revisiting your decision in a few months or a few years.

Yet in order to take that next step, you have to lift your foot from a place where the footing is sure and step into some uncertainty. The poet T. S. Eliot puts it this way:

> What we call the beginning is often the end
> And to make an end is to make a beginning.
> The end is where we start from.
>   ...And any action
> Is a step to the block, to the fire, down the sea's throat
> Or to an illegible stone: and that is where we start.[2]

Every step is a step in faith. When your path seems frightening and lonely and the way is unclear, remember that there really are people out there, in the church, in the seminary, among your friends and family, who can give you guidance and support; and that in the times of greatest uncertainty God goes with you.

NOTES

Chapter III

1. Malcolm Warford, *Our Several Callings: A Foundation Paper on Vocation as a Lifelong Issue for Education* (Cleveland: Division of Education and Publication, United Church Board for Homeland Ministries, 1990), 10.

2. Marjorie Grene, ed., *Knowing and Being: Essays by Michael Polanyi* (Chicago: University of Chicago Press, 1969), 133.

3. Quoted in Lovett H. Weems, Jr., "Toward Building a Passionate Ministry," *Circuit Rider* (July/August, 1989): 11.

4. Elizabeth O'Connor, *Eighth Day of Creation: Gifts and Creativity* (Waco, Texas: Word Books, 1971), 14.

5. Walter Brueggemann, "Covenanting as Human Vocation: A Discussion of the Relations of Bible and Pastoral Care," *Interpretation*, XXXIII, 2, April 1979, 125.

6. *Ibid.*, 126.

7. Lewis Hyde, *The Gift: Imagination and the Erotic Life of Property*, (New York: Vintage Books, 1979), 4.

8. Elizabeth O'Connor, *The New Community* (New York: Harper and Row, 1976), 101.

9. Fredrick Buechner, *Wishful Thinking: A Theological ABC* (New York: Harper and Row, 1973), 95.

10. *Eighth Day of Creation*, 55.

11. T. S. Eliot, *Four Quartets* (New York: Harcourt Brace Jovanovich, 1943), 59.

12. Alton Beaver, ed., *The Call and Nurture of Ministers: A Manual*

for Church Elders (Published by Phillips Graduate Seminary in Coopera-
tion with the Christian Church [Disciples of Christ] in Oklahoma, 1992), 8.
    13. *Ibid.*, 6.

Chapter IV

    1. "Procedures, Standards, and Criteria for Membership," *Bulletin*,
42, part 3, 1996 (The Association of Theological Schools): 75-113
passim.

Chapter VI

    1. Jacob Needleman, *Money and the Meaning of Life* (New York:
Doubleday, 1991), 269.

Chapter VII

    1. Marvin J. Taylor, ed., *Fact Book on Theological Education,
1973-74* (Vandalia, Ohio: American Association of Theological Schools,
1974), 5.
    2. Jonathan Strom and Daniel Aleshire, eds., *Fact Book of Theologi-
cal Education, 1996-97* (Pittsburgh: The Association of Theological
Schools, 1997), 41.
    3. Patricia M. Y. Chang, "Female Clergy in the Contemporary
Protestant Church: A Current Assessment," *Journal for the Scientific
Study of Religion*, 36, no. 4 (Dec. 1997): 568.
    4. *Ibid.*, 568.
    5. *The United Methodist Newscope* 25, no. 43 (Oct. 24, 1997): 3.
    6. AAPC website (http://www.metanoia.org/aapc).
    7. American Association of Pastoral Counselors, 9504A Lee High-
way, Fairfax, Virginia 22031-2303, Phone: (703) 385-6967, Fax: (703)
352-7725.

Chapter VIII

1. *Our Several Callings*, 23-24.
2. *Four Quartets*, 58.